The Kids Book of Canadian
Prime Ministers

WRITTEN BY
Pat Hancock

ILLUSTRATED BY
John Mantha

KIDS CAN PRESS

Acknowledgements

Special thanks to the Kids Can team for their high standards of editing, fact checking
and design, and for their inspired choice of John Mantha as illustrator.

Text copyright © 1998 by Pat Hancock
Illustrations copyright © 1998 by John Mantha

We acknowledge the support of the Canada Council for the Arts
and the Ontario Arts Council for our publishing program.

Published in Canada by
Kids Can Press Ltd.
29 Birch Avenue
Toronto, ON M4V 1E2

Published in the U.S. by
Kids Can Press Ltd.
85 River Rock Drive, Suite 202
Buffalo, NY 14207

Edited by Elizabeth MacLeod
Designed by Marie Bartholomew and Julia Naimska
Printed in Hong Kong by Wing King Tong Co. Ltd.

CM 98 0 9 8 7 6 5 4 3 2 1

Canadian Cataloging in Publication Data

Hancock, Pat
The Kids book of Canadian prime ministers

Includes index.
ISBN 1-55074-473-9

1. Prime ministers — Canada — Biography — Juvenile literature. I. Mantha, John. II. Title.

FC26.P7H36 1998   j971.009'9   C98-930467-1
F1005.H36 1998

Contents

Canada's Government 4

The Government at Work 6

Sir John Alexander Macdonald 8

Alexander Mackenzie 13

Sir John Joseph Caldwell Abbott 15

Sir John Sparrow David Thompson 16

Sir Mackenzie Bowell 17

Sir Charles Tupper 18

Sir Wilfrid Laurier 19

Sir Robert Laird Borden 23

Arthur Meighen 25

William Lyon Mackenzie King 26

Richard Bedford Bennett 31

Louis Stephen St. Laurent 33

John George Diefenbaker 35

Lester Bowles Pearson 37

Pierre Elliott Trudeau 39

Charles Joseph Clark 44

John Napier Turner 45

Martin Brian Mulroney 46

Avril Kim Campbell 50

Joseph Jacques Jean Chrétien 51

Time Line 53

Index 54

Canada's Government

The prime minister is the leader of Canada's government.
But what kind of government does the PM lead, and how does he get to lead it?

A Representative Democracy

Canada is a democracy, which means that Canadians govern themselves, or run their own country. But millions of Canadians can't vote every time a decision must be made. It would take forever to get anything done that way. So they choose people to represent them and make decisions on their behalf. These representatives make decisions about running the country in Parliament in Ottawa. That's why they are called members of Parliament (MPs).

Federal Elections

MPs are chosen in country-wide, or federal, elections. The country is divided into voting regions called ridings, and at election time, the person who gets the most votes in a riding becomes the MP.

Most people who want to be MPs belong to political parties, such as the Liberal Party and the Progressive Conservative Party. These parties are made up of people who share the same ideas about how to run Canada. After an election, MPs from the party with the most elected members form the government, and their party's leader becomes prime minister.

Head of State

The prime minister is the leader of the government (page 6), but Canada also has a head of state. The head of state symbolizes the whole country, its people and its laws. In Canada that person is the British monarch (Queen or King), represented by the governor general.

The governor general acts as Canada's head of state. She is not elected to this position. The prime minister appoints her so that she will represent everyone, not just the people who would vote for her. The governor general follows the wishes of Canadians by approving, or giving "royal assent" to, the elected government's decisions.

The Houses of Parliament

Parliament is divided into two parts: the House of Commons and the Senate, both located in the Parliament Buildings in Ottawa. MPs elected from all across the country sit in the House of Commons, which currently has 301 seats — one for each riding.

It is to the House that the government, with its majority of MPs, presents its plans for running the country. MPs belonging to the party with the next largest number of elected members form the official Opposition in the House. Their job is to study the government's plans very carefully, and to ask tough questions about the new laws, or legislation, the government wants the House to approve.

If the House of Commons votes to approve these plans, the government then presents them to the Senate, which currently has 104 members. The prime minister appoints senators from all regions of the country, and they may keep their seats until they reach age 75. Their job is to take a careful, second look at government plans that have been approved by the House of Commons.

The Cabinet

The prime minister gives some MPs special jobs, or portfolios. These MPs are called ministers and are in charge of the main government departments, also called ministries, such as Finance, Citizenship and Immigration, and Health. These ministers and the prime minister form what is called the Cabinet. The Cabinet may also include a few advisers who aren't in charge of a particular department. They're called ministers without portfolios.

The Government at Work

Getting Down to Business

The prime minister and Cabinet usually decide what new laws the government would like to make. Cabinet members present MPs in the House of Commons with detailed plans for the proposed new laws, called bills. These bills are studied, discussed and debated by MPs and defended by Cabinet members.

Each bill is read, or studied carefully, three times by the House before MPs finally vote on it and send it on to the Senate. After their debate on a bill, the senators either pass it in the form it is in or send it back to the House with some changes. MPs must vote to approve or reject any changes proposed by the Senate.

Once a bill gets final approval in the House, it goes to the governor general for royal assent. Then, and only then, does it become a new law, or act, governing all Canadians.

Going to the People

In Canada, a federal election must be held at least every five years. If people don't like the bills passed by the government, or the way their MPs represent them in the House of Commons, they can vote for new representatives in the next election. Regular elections, together with the careful process of studying a bill many times before it becomes law, help make the government responsible to the people of Canada.

What the Prime Minister Does

The prime minister's role and powers aren't described in the Constitution. But this doesn't mean that a prime minister can do whatever he wants. Generally, he follows the traditions of Parliament, doing what prime ministers have always done. The job includes:

• Government Leader

The PM's main job is to lead the government. This involves speaking in Parliament, to the media, at national meetings such as premiers' conferences, and at international gatherings of government leaders. The PM also decides which bills Cabinet members bring before the House of Commons. He appoints senators, chooses governors general and provincial lieutenant-governors, and appoints judges to the Supreme Court and federal courts.

The Senate

House of Commons

• Cabinet Leader

After choosing the Cabinet ministers who will run the government departments, the prime minister must also make sure they do a good job. He does this by holding regular Cabinet meetings. What goes on at these meetings is kept secret, so it's hard to know exactly how a prime minister handles this part of the job. But it is in these meetings that Cabinet ministers must get the PM's approval before presenting new bills in the House. A minister who loses the PM's approval soon loses a place at the Cabinet table.

• Member of Parliament

A prime minister must also be an MP in order to sit in the House of Commons. So the PM also has the responsibility of representing the interests of the riding that elected him to the House.

• Party Leader

To lead Canada, a prime minister must first win the leadership of a political party. But once in office, the PM must work to serve the best interests of the country, even if it means disagreeing with his party's wishes. Still, as party leader, the prime minister also hosts or attends party meetings and fund-raising events, and works to keep the party well organized between elections.

• International Leader

As leader of one of the most respected democracies, Canada's prime minister also serves as a world leader. In peaceful times and during times of crisis, the PM's opinions and decisions can influence the political, economic and social decisions other countries make.

SIR John Alexander Macdonald

In 1833 lawyer John Alexander Macdonald came to Hallowell (now Picton, Ontario) to help with his sick cousin's law practice. Macdonald could afford a new suit and boots, but not a horse and buggy. So every day he set out along the dirt road, carrying his new jacket and boots. Just outside town, he'd brush off the dust, slip into his new clothes, and walk smartly into Hallowell. Each evening, he did the same in reverse. Still short of money and still a lover of fashionable clothes, 34 years later Macdonald would stand proudly in front of Governor General Lord Monck to be sworn in as Canada's first prime minister.

Quick Facts

Born: Jan. 11, 1815, at Glasgow, Scotland

Politics: Liberal-Conservative (now Conservative)

Married: Isabella Clark, 1843 (two sons, one died); widowed, 1857; married Susan Agnes Bernard, 1867 (one daughter)

Occupation: lawyer

Political Positions: elected to Province of Canada's Legislative Assembly for Kingston, Canada West (Ontario), 1844; joint premier of Province of Canada, 1856–62 and 1864–67; leader of Liberal-Conservatives, 1867–91; MP for Kingston, ON, 1867–78 and 1887–91; leader of Opposition, 1873–78; MP for Victoria, BC, 1878–82; MP for Carleton, ON, 1882–87

Prime Minister: July 1, 1867–Nov. 5, 1873; Oct. 17, 1878–June 6, 1891

Died: June 6, 1891, at Ottawa, ON

Friendly and Popular

Smart and hard-working, Macdonald became known as a brilliant lawyer. He was also quick with a joke, had an amazing memory for names and faces, and impressed people as a down-to-earth man who cared about them. But Macdonald had to cope with a lot. His first wife, Isabella, was very sick, and their first son died just after his first birthday. As well, politics took Macdonald away from his law practice — his main source of income — and he often was broke. His habit of turning to alcohol to forget his troubles eventually became public knowledge, and was occasionally used against him. But, election after election, voters overlooked it and gave Macdonald their support.

A Divided Canada

From the time he was elected to the legislature of the Province of Canada, Macdonald worked hard to unite the various political groups called Conservatives. In 1856 he became their leader, but they were still divided, representing mainly English-speaking residents of Canada West (Ontario). Macdonald knew his party must gain support in Canada East (Quebec). So he joined forces with Canada East's Conservative leader, Étienne-Paschal Taché, and they became co-premiers of Canada. But Canadians continued to quarrel about religion (Catholic vs. Protestant) and language (French vs. English), making it very difficult for the government to do a good job.

Father of Confederation

By early 1864 Macdonald was so fed up with the squabbling that he was ready to resign as leader. But his hope for a strong, united Canada was suddenly renewed. That summer and fall, leaders from Canada East and West (Quebec and Ontario), Nova Scotia, New Brunswick and Prince Edward Island met in Charlottetown, Halifax and Quebec City to discuss becoming a country. From late 1864 to the winter of 1867, Macdonald worked hard to shape the new country. He insisted on a strong central government with only certain provincial powers. P.E.I. disagreed and remained a British colony (so did Newfoundland). But the Province of Canada, Nova Scotia and New Brunswick agreed, and on July 1, 1867, the Dominion of Canada was born, with Macdonald as prime minister. To honour him for uniting the country, Queen Victoria made him Sir John.

> "WHATEVER YOU DO, ADHERE TO THE UNION. WE ARE A GREAT COUNTRY, AND SHALL BECOME ONE OF THE GREATEST IN THE UNIVERSE IF WE PRESERVE IT; WE SHALL SINK INTO INSIGNIFICANCE AND ADVERSITY IF WE SUFFER IT TO BE BROKEN."
>
> *Macdonald, 1861*

The Fathers of Confederation. Macdonald is sitting in the middle.

Louis Riel

Macdonald made a big mistake when Canada took over the North-West Territories. He never bothered to ask the settlers living there if they wanted to become part of Canada. In December 1869 Louis Riel, leader of the French-speaking Métis (people of Aboriginal and European descent) in the area, formed a government and organized what became known as the Red River Rebellion to fight Canada's take-over plans.

When Thomas Scott, a man from Ontario was captured and executed by the Métis, many furious Ontario Conservatives wanted Riel punished for Scott's death. But Macdonald's government negotiated with Riel's government instead, and the new province of Manitoba was formed in July 1870.

In 1885, trouble was brewing in the West again, mainly because Macdonald was ignoring the needs and rights of people living in what is now Saskatchewan. Once more, Riel led settlers in rebellion. However, this time, he was tried for treason and sentenced to death.

To French Catholics in Quebec, Riel was a hero. To Ontario's Protestants, he was Scott's murderer. And to Aboriginal people and Métis, he was a brave leader. Riel was now mentally ill, and many legal experts argued that he should not be executed. But Macdonald let the sentence be carried out at Regina on November 16, 1885. The angry reaction to Riel's death still echoes in Quebec and among Métis.

The North-West Territories

In March 1867 the United States bought Alaska from Russia. Britain worried that the U.S. would next try to buy Rupert's Land — the lands around all the rivers draining into Hudson Bay — and the North-Western Territory. The Hudson's Bay

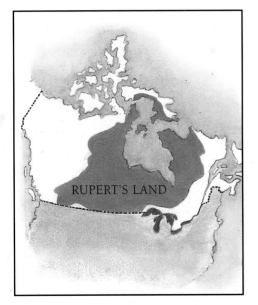

Company controlled the land, but agreed to sell it to the Canadian government. In July 1870, this vast area joined Canada.

Promising a Rail Link

Macdonald worried that Canada might lose British Columbia to the Americans. So his government agreed to take over B.C.'s debt and build a railway to the Pacific by 1881. B.C. joined Canada on July 20, 1871. P.E.I. followed in 1873.

The Pacific Railway Scandal

Macdonald now had to raise money for a cross-Canada railway and for the 1872 election campaign. Sir Hugh Allan wanted his company to get the contract to build the Canadian Pacific Railway, so he gave the Conservatives $350 000, hoping that would win him the rail business. Macdonald's government was re-elected in 1872. But in spring 1873, a telegram Sir John sent to Allan during the 1872 campaign fell into Liberal hands. In it, Macdonald pleaded, "I must have another ten thousand. Will be the last time of

calling. Do not fail me. Answer me today." Facing charges of bribery and corruption, Sir John's government resigned.

Back in Power

Macdonald campaigned hard when the Liberals called an election in 1878. He promised new taxes on American goods to protect Canadian businesses and farmers. The Conservatives won the election and Sir John was PM again.

A Proud Finish

One of Sir John's proudest moments occurred on April 29, 1891, when he escorted his son, Hugh John Macdonald, into the House of Commons as a new MP. A month later, Sir John suffered a stroke and died on June 6, 1891.

From Sea to Sea

Macdonald's dream of a Canada united by rail came true when the last spike was driven into the tracks at Craigellachie, BC, on November 7, 1885. The next summer, Sir John and his wife rode the train all the way to the Pacific.

OTHER MILESTONES

- made it legal for workers to form trade unions, 1872
- *formed the North-West Mounted Police (now the RCMP), 1873*
- created Canada's first national park at Banff, AB, 1885

THE OLD FLAG, THE OLD POLICY, THE OLD LEADER.

Alexander Mackenzie

Sandy Mackenzie was earning a decent living as a stonemason in Scotland, but unemployment was growing. As well, his childhood sweetheart, Helen Neil, decided to move to Canada with her parents. So in April 1842 Mackenzie packed up his tools and sailed with the Neils. Not for an instant did he imagine that, 31 years later, he would become Canada's second prime minister.

Entering Politics

After a few years in Kingston, Mackenzie moved to Sarnia, where he set up a building company. When a provincial election was called in 1861, local voters saw him as a sensible, hard-working and honest candidate and elected him. They also elected him to Canada's first Parliament in 1867.

Quick Facts

Born: Jan. 28, 1822, near Dunkeld, Scotland

Politics: Liberal

Married: Helen Neil, 1845 (three children, one survived); widowed, 1852; married Jane Sym, 1853

Occupation: stonemason, businessman

Political Positions: elected to Province of Canada's Legislative Assembly for Lambton, Canada West (Ontario), 1861; MP for Lambton, ON, 1867–82; leader of Liberals, 1873–80; MP for York East, ON, 1882–92

Prime Minister: Nov. 7, 1873–Oct. 8, 1878

Died: Apr. 17, 1892, at Toronto, ON

Time to Govern

Mackenzie was Liberal leader in 1873 when Sir John A. Macdonald's Conservative government resigned because of the Pacific Scandal (page 11). Governor General Lord Dufferin asked Mackenzie and his Liberals to take over, and suddenly, Sandy Mackenzie was Canada's new PM.

Liberals in Power

Mackenzie wanted to give the people a chance to vote on their new government, so he called an election two months later. He promised to stop borrowing money to finish building the transcontinental railway, and said he would lower the special taxes, called tariffs, that made goods coming from the U.S. more expensive than Canadian goods. He also promised to run an honest government. Fed up with the Conservatives, voters elected their first Liberal government.

Taxing Problems

When Mackenzie cut back on railway building, people in British Columbia complained that Canada wasn't keeping its Confederation promise to connect the country by rail. To raise more money to run the country, Mackenzie had to increase the tariffs he had promised to lower. That angered many Liberals who believed in free trade, without special taxes, between Canada and the U.S. Conservatives were angry because they felt Mackenzie hadn't raised the tariffs enough. They wanted American goods to be as expensive as possible so Canadians would buy Canadian products.

Conservative Comeback

In Canada and around the world in the late 1870s, prices fell for such things as timber, fish and grain. Businesses closed and jobs were hard to find. People wanted the government to solve these problems. As the next election grew nearer, Opposition leader Sir John A. Macdonald saw his big chance. He promised "A Canada for Canadians," with high protective tariffs and a completed railway. In September 1878 Macdonald's Conservatives surged back into power. Devastated, Mackenzie resigned as PM. He stayed on as Opposition leader for two more years.

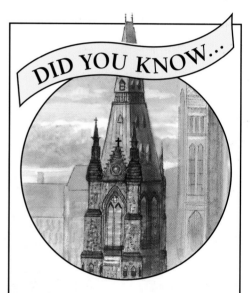

OTHER MILESTONES

- *passed a law bringing in the secret ballot, 1874*
- made the North-West Mounted Police the official police force in Canada's west, 1874
- set up Canada's first Supreme Court, 1875
- appointed Canada's first auditor general, the person who watches carefully over how the government spends money, 1878

"ALEXANDER MACKENZIE WAS STRAIGHT AND SOLID AS OLD MASONRY … IT WOULD BE WELL IF WE HAD MORE MACKENZIES IN PUBLIC LIFE TODAY."

Wilfrid Laurier, 1892

SIR John Joseph Caldwell Abbott

Sir John A. Macdonald was dying. As the sad news spread, people wondered who would take his place. Many Conservatives agreed that John Thompson, Sir John's brilliant minister of Justice, would do the job well. While French-speaking Catholics in Quebec were pleased that Thompson was a Roman Catholic, many of Ontario's Protestant Conservatives weren't. To avoid a major split in his party, Thompson recommended that John Abbott, a Protestant, be chosen instead.

Doing His Duty

Abbott was a senator when he became PM. He was 70 years old and sickly. Two days before Sir John died, he wrote to a friend, "Why should I go where the doing of honest work will only make me hated?" But his party needed him, so he went.

In Power

Abbott hoped his party would soon choose another leader, so he planned no major changes. But he did what he could to end scandals and bribery in the government, and he worked with John Thompson to shape hundreds of Canada's laws into a clear, organized code of crimes and matching punishments.

> "I AM HERE VERY MUCH BECAUSE I AM NOT PARTICULARLY OBNOXIOUS TO ANYONE."
>
> Abbott, 1891

In Poor Health

Because he was a senator and not an MP, Abbott couldn't sit in the House of Commons, so he left much of the daily running of the government to Thompson. Despite that, by July 1892 Abbott's health became worse. His doctor ordered rest, but it didn't help. On November 24, 1892, he resigned as PM.

Quick Facts

Born: Mar. 12, 1821, at St. Andrews East, Lower Canada

Politics: Liberal-Conservative (now Conservative)

Married: Mary Bethune, 1849 (eight children)

Occupation: lawyer

Political Positions: MP for Argenteuil, PQ, 1867–74, 1881–87; senator, 1887–93; mayor of Montreal, 1887–89; leader of Liberal-Conservatives, 1891–92

Prime Minister: June 16, 1891–Nov. 24, 1892

Died: Oct. 30, 1893, at Montreal, PQ

SIR John Sparrow David Thompson

All John Thompson ever wanted was to be a judge. So even though he had been his province's premier, he happily gave up politics when he was appointed to the Nova Scotia Supreme Court in 1882. Thompson loved his job, and did it superbly. He also liked the regular court hours that let him spend time with his family. So Conservative friends and his wife, Annie, had to push him to answer Sir John A. Macdonald's call to come to Ottawa in 1885.

Quick Facts

Born: Nov. 10, 1845, at Halifax, NS

Politics: Liberal-Conservative (now Conservative)

Married: Annie Affleck, 1870 (nine children, five survived infancy)

Occupation: lawyer

Political Positions: premier of Nova Scotia, 1882; MP for Antigonish, NS, 1885–94; leader of the Liberal-Conservatives, 1892–94

Prime Minister: Dec. 5, 1892–Dec. 12, 1894

Died: Dec. 12, 1894, at Windsor Castle, England

Justice for All

Macdonald made Thompson minister of Justice. Thompson soon settled two tricky fishing and sealing disputes between Canada and the U.S. He also set up a criminal code for Canada, the first of its kind in the world. It carefully described all the actions considered crimes in Canada and suitable matching punishments. It also gave judges some flexibility when dealing with offenders, especially those under age 16. Parliament passed the Criminal Code bill in 1892.

PM Thompson

In 1892 Thompson was also busy doing much of PM Abbott's work because the new PM didn't have a seat in the House of Commons. When ill health forced Abbott to resign, Thompson agreed to become prime minister.

Canada's Loss

Thompson's accomplishments impressed Queen Victoria. In 1894 she invited him to London to be sworn in as a special adviser. Thompson wanted to take Annie with him, but he could barely afford the uniform he needed for the ceremony. Sadly, as he sat down to lunch with the Queen, he had a heart attack and died.

SIR Mackenzie Bowell

Mackenzie Bowell was just 11 when he was sent to work at the *Belleville Intelligencer* newspaper. He started as a printer's devil, the nickname given to boys and girls who got covered with black ink pulling freshly printed sheets of paper off the presses. From printer's devil to editor to newspaper owner, Bowell worked his way to the top. From 1867 on, he was a popular local member of Parliament, winning election after election until 1892 when he was appointed to the Senate. However, he wasn't as popular in the government because he was often seen as extremely anti-Catholic and anti-Liberal.

Next in Line

Sir John A. Macdonald had died in 1891 and in 1894 Conservatives were still feeling the loss. Now they and the governor general had to find the third government leader in three years. The job became Bowell's.

In the Hot Seat

Bowell's party turned against him when he became PM. Many didn't like his extreme views on religion. But when he tried to be fair to Manitoba's French-speaking Catholics by passing a bill to make the province give them back their own schools, several of his Cabinet ministers resigned in protest. Seeing himself in "a nest of traitors," as he put it, he resigned too. Canada again had no PM.

Quick Facts

Born: Dec. 27, 1823, at Rickinghall, England

Politics: Liberal-Conservative (now Conservative)

Married: Harriet Moore, 1847 (nine children)

Occupation: newspaper owner

Political Positions: MP for North Hastings, ON, 1867–92; senator, 1892–1917; leader of Liberal-Conservatives, 1894–96

Prime Minister: Dec. 21, 1894–Apr. 27, 1896

Died: Dec. 10, 1917, at Belleville, ON

DID YOU KNOW...

... Bowell was the second — and last — senator to be prime minister? Today, if a PM resigned, the deputy-PM would likely take over until the party chose a new leader.

SIR Charles Tupper

Charles Tupper was a Father of Confederation, one of the leaders who shaped the new Dominion of Canada (page 9). He fought long and hard to convince Nova Scotians they would be better off in Confederation. And without him, Sir John A. Macdonald might not have been able to keep Nova Scotians in Canada when they almost changed their minds right after joining.

Quick Facts

Born: July 2, 1821, at Amherst, NS

Politics: Conservative

Married: Frances Morse, 1846 (six children)

Occupation: doctor

Political Positions: elected to the Nova Scotia Legislative Assembly, 1855; premier of Nova Scotia, 1864–67; MP for Cumberland, NS, 1867–84, 1887–88; MP for Cape Breton, NS, 1896–1900; leader of the Conservatives, 1896–1901

Prime Minister: May 1, 1896–July 8, 1896

Died: Oct. 30, 1915, at Bexley Heath, England

Working for Canada

Tupper was very important in Macdonald's governments. Tupper made an agreement with Louis Riel (page 10) that led to Manitoba joining Canada, and as the Cabinet minister in charge of railways (1879–1884), he made sure that the Canadian Pacific Railway was finally built.

Waiting His Turn

Some thought Tupper would replace Macdonald when he died, but Abbott got the job. Tupper was also passed over for Thompson and Bowell. He returned from England, where he was Canada's representative, to take part in the Cabinet revolt that forced Bowell to resign (page 17). Tupper finally became PM in 1896.

In and Out of Office

The government had been in power for five years, so Tupper had to call an election. Conservatives were split over the Manitoba schools issue (page 21), and they were up against a popular Liberal leader, Wilfrid Laurier. The Liberals won, and Tupper had to resign.

DID YOU KNOW...

... Tupper's 69 days is the shortest term of all prime ministers?

SIR Wilfrid Laurier

It was obvious to Wilfrid Laurier's professors and friends at McGill University that he would go far. Handsome and charming, he spoke French and English fluently, and wasn't afraid to speak his mind. He also managed to earn top marks while holding down a part-time job as a law clerk. Not surprisingly, he was chosen valedictorian for his graduating class. Years later, he would speak for all of Canada.

> "CANADA HAS BEEN THE INSPIRATION OF MY LIFE."
>
> *Laurier, 1911*

Quick Facts

Born: Nov. 20, 1841, at St. Lin, Canada East (now Quebec)

Politics: Liberal

Married: Zoê Lafontaine, 1868 (no children)

Occupation: lawyer

Political Positions: member of Quebec Legislative Assembly, 1871–74; MP for Drummond-Arthabaska, PQ, 1874–77; MP for Quebec East, 1877–1919; leader of Liberals, 1887–1919; leader of Opposition, 1887–96, 1911–19

Prime Minister: July 11, 1896–Oct. 6, 1911

Died: Feb. 17, 1919, at Ottawa, ON

Coming of Age

The Laurier years were exciting times for Canada. Thousands of immigrants settled in the west, turning much of the prairies into wheat fields. Gold and other minerals were mined in the north, and two new trans-Canada railways were begun. But good times also brought problems. Many people had to work long hours for very low wages in unsafe factories. To help settle strikes and improve working conditions, Laurier set up Canada's first department of Labour.

In the early 1900s, Britain wanted to take charge of making British Empire countries, including Canada, work together more. But Laurier argued that Canada could make its own decisions, and that Britain should treat these countries as free nations. Laurier set up the first department of External Affairs so Canada could gather its own information — not just information from Britain — on what was happening in the rest of the world.

In 1910 Laurier's government passed a bill to establish the Royal Canadian Navy. Because it had only a few ships at first, many English Canadians made fun of it, calling it a tin pot navy. Many French Canadians thought it was just another attempt to help England fight its wars. But for Laurier, it was a sign of Canada's growing independence. Laurier also encouraged exploration in the Arctic and sent the North-West Mounted Police to the area to prevent the United States from claiming the land east of Alaska.

Entering Politics

Laurier quickly earned a reputation as an excellent lawyer and public speaker. When he ran for a seat in the Quebec legislature in 1871, he made it clear that he felt people should be free to vote however they wanted. That didn't please some powerful Catholic church leaders in Quebec. They told Catholics not to vote for free-thinking Liberals, such as Laurier. But Catholics and English-speaking Protestants voted for him anyway. In 1874 he was elected as an MP. Thirteen years later he became Liberal leader. After years in Opposition, Laurier's Liberals finally defeated the Conservatives in 1896, and Laurier became prime minister.

A Balancing Act

Laurier was proud to be Canada's first French-speaking PM. He dreamed of a united Canada, a country no longer divided along language and religious lines. During the election campaign, he had promised to find a compromise to deal with the closing of Manitoba's Catholic schools. As PM, Laurier worked out an arrangement that allowed religion to be taught at the end of the school day and French classes where there were enough French-speaking students. French Catholics thought Laurier hadn't done enough, and Manitoba later rejected the deal. But Laurier had calmed things down for a while.

Whose War Is It?

In 1899 Britain wanted Canadian soldiers to help fight the Boer War in South Africa. Laurier agreed to pay the costs of men who volunteered, but refused to force Canadians to fight. Many English Canadians thought that wasn't enough, while many French Canadians thought Canada should never help England fight its wars.

Yukon Gold and Prairie Wheat

In 1896 gold was discovered in the Klondike, and people rushed north to find their fortunes. Laurier's government also encouraged people to go west by offering settlers free land in exchange for setting up homesteads. Thousands of hard-working families arrived from Europe to begin new lives, many as prairie wheat farmers.

Losing Power

In 1910 nearly 8000 farmers marched on Ottawa to demand better wheat prices. The next year, Laurier worked out a trade deal with the U.S. that helped farmers, but annoyed eastern business owners. Conservatives who opposed free trade were furious. They vowed to defeat Laurier and the trade plans. In the 1911 election campaign, they fought against "trade with the Yankees" and "a tin pot navy" — and won.

In Opposition

Laurier's passionate speeches as Opposition leader often made life difficult for the new PM, Robert Borden. But during World War I, Laurier worked with Borden to support Canada's war efforts. And in 1916 he supported Borden's Union Government so that Canadians wouldn't have to fight an election as well as a war. However, in 1917 Borden introduced a plan to conscript, or force, men to serve in the army. Knowing how much most French Canadians hated the idea of conscription, Laurier opposed the bill. Many English Canadians were furious. In the 1917 election, the Liberals were defeated everywhere but in Quebec. Deeply saddened, Laurier stayed on in Opposition until his death in 1919.

OTHER MILESTONES

- *established the Yukon Territory, with Dawson as its capital, 1898*
- *Saskatchewan and Alberta joined Confederation, 1905*

SIR Robert Laird Borden

Robert Laird Borden's farm chores kept him away from school when he was young. But Borden was able to study at home. By the time he was 14, he was going to school regularly — as a teacher. Six years later, he became a law clerk, and ended up as head of one of Nova Scotia's finest law firms. He also became an MP, a bank president and an author. He replaced Sir Charles Tupper as Conservative leader and became PM during one of Canada's most difficult periods.

Gaining Power

After losing to Laurier in 1904, Borden was determined to find the weak spots in Laurier's popularity. By 1911 he had found them. Both French and English Canadians were angry about Laurier's navy plans (page 20), and Borden used that anger to drive a wedge between Liberal supporters. He also fed the old fears of Canadians about being taken over by the U.S. when he spoke against the reciprocity (free-trade) treaty. His divide-and-conquer approach worked. He was in, Laurier was out, the trade deal was off, and plans for supporting a Canadian navy were put on hold.

> "HE SERVED HIS COUNTRY WELL."
> Arthur Meighen, 1960

DID YOU KNOW...

... Borden's portrait is on the $100 bill?

Quick Facts

Born: June 26, 1854, at Grand Pré, NS

Politics: Conservative

Married: Laura Bond, 1889 (no children)

Occupation: teacher, lawyer

Political Positions: MP for Halifax, NS, 1896–1904; leader of Conservatives, 1901–20; MP for Carleton, ON, 1905–08; MP for Halifax, NS, 1908–17; MP for King's County, NS, 1917–20

Prime Minister: Oct. 10, 1911–July 10, 1920

Died: June 10, 1937, at Ottawa, ON

OTHER MILESTONES
• after the war, encouraged the formation of the League of Nations, an organization of member countries working together for peace and security
• set up the Employment Service of Canada to help people find jobs, 1919

Canada at War, 1914–1918

When Britain declared war against Germany in August 1914, Canada was at war too, and Canadians united behind Borden. He brought in the Emergency War Measures Act, which allowed the government to make decisions quickly, without Parliament's approval. When he announced that Canada would send half a million soldiers to Europe, thousands and thousands of young men volunteered. Borden raised money for the war effort by taxing the profits of companies making war supplies. In 1917 he brought in Canada's first income tax. It was supposed to be temporary.

On the Home Front

Some people got rich by selling the government poorly made guns, boots, bullets and shells. Such schemes cost soldiers their lives, and Borden was blamed. He was criticized even more when his decision to bring in conscription in 1917 tore the country apart (page 22). But Borden was praised for the way he dealt with Britain during the war. In 1917 he convinced Britain that Canada and other British Commonwealth countries must be treated as equal partners, not as colonies under British control. Canada's prime minister had become a world leader.

Voting Rights

Before calling the 1917 election, Borden gave the right to vote to women in the armed forces, as well as to the wives, mothers, daughters and widows of servicemen. But he took away the voting rights of many

immigrants who came to Canada after 1902. Then he led a union of pro-conscription Conservatives and Liberals to victory over Laurier.

Leading a Union Government

Troubles awaited Borden's Union Government. After many protests, Borden finally gave all women over 21 the right to vote in 1918. In May 1919, over 30 000 workers shut down Winnipeg during the country's first general strike. The government's decision to send the Royal Canadian Mounted Police to force them back to work left many workers furious. In 1920, sick and exhausted, Borden quit as PM.

The Winnipeg General Strike

Arthur Meighen

Like Borden, the prime minister he replaced, Arthur Meighen was a poor farm boy who worked hard for everything he got. He had a sharp mind and an amazing memory — he could recite long passages from Shakespeare by heart. Meighen also loved debating and was good at it. But, as he quickly learned when he became PM, actions speak louder than words.

An Unpopular Leader

As the Conservatives' new leader, Meighen wasn't popular with voters in 1920. He had angered many French Canadians by supporting conscription (page 22). He had recommended using force to end the Winnipeg strike (page 24). His plan to form the Canadian National Railways (CNR) by taking over some private railways in 1919 looked to many like a scheme to make a few rich railway owners richer. And unhappy farmers were joining a new political party — the Progressive Party.

Down to Defeat

Still, Meighen battled on. During the December 1921 election campaign, Conservatives said, "Canada needs Meighen." But a majority of Canadians disagreed and voted for Mackenzie King's Liberals.

A Brief Comeback

In 1926 scandals about liquor smuggling forced the Liberals to resign. Meighen became PM again, but his new government lasted only a few months. Meighen tried a comeback in 1942, but didn't even get elected as an MP.

> ### Quick Facts
>
> Born: June 16, 1874, at Anderson, ON
>
> Politics: Conservative
>
> Married: Isabel J. Cox, 1904 (three children)
>
> Occupation: teacher, lawyer
>
> Political Positions: MP for Portage la Prairie, MB, 1908–21, 1925–26; MP for Grenville, ON, 1922–25; leader of Conservatives, 1920–26, 1941–42; senator, 1932–42
>
> Prime Minister: July 10, 1920–Dec. 29, 1921; June 29, 1926–Sept. 25, 1926
>
> Died: Aug. 5, 1960 at Toronto, ON

Canada's tenth prime minister

William Lyon Mackenzie King

Young "Willie" King grew up hearing stories about the grandfather he was named after. His mother told him about how her father, William Lyon Mackenzie, led the Rebellion of 1837 in Upper Canada (now Ontario), how he managed to escape to the United States, and how he returned to Canada after being pardoned to become Toronto's first mayor. Mackenzie King grew up thinking about how he too could serve his country.

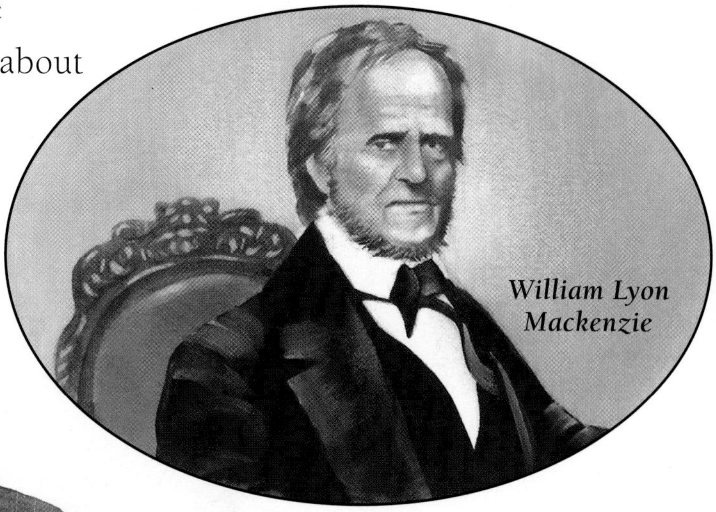

William Lyon Mackenzie

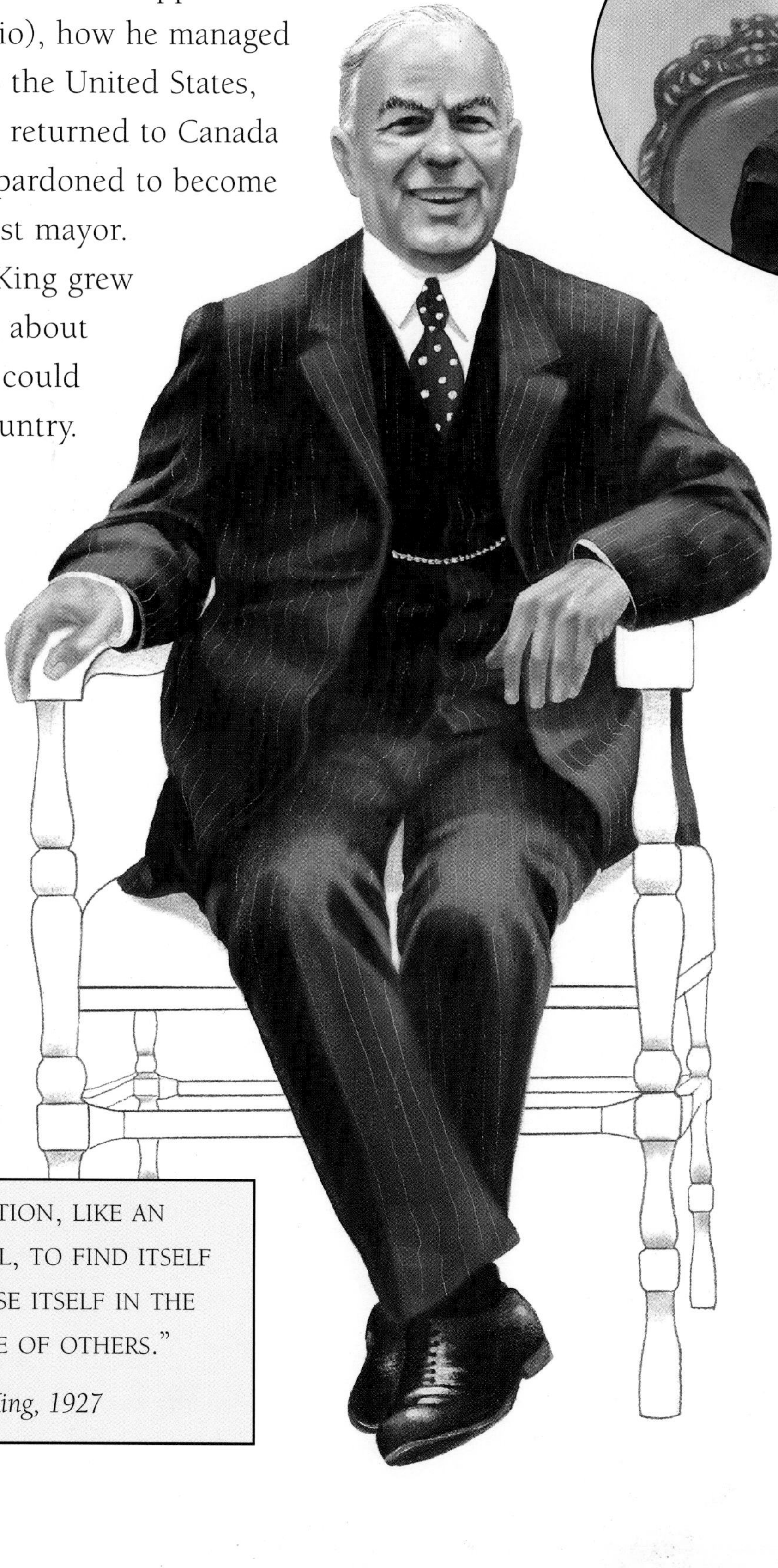

Quick Facts

Born: Dec. 17, 1874, at Berlin (now Kitchener), ON

Politics: Liberal

Occupation: lawyer, civil servant

Political Positions: MP for Waterloo North, ON, 1908–11; MP for Prince, PEI, 1919–21; leader of Liberals, 1919–48; MP for York North, ON, 1921–25; MP for Prince Albert, SK, 1926–45; MP for Glengarry, ON, 1945–49

Prime Minister: Dec. 29, 1921–June 28, 1926; Sept. 25, 1926–Aug. 7, 1930; Oct. 23, 1935–Nov. 15, 1948

Died: July 22, 1950, at Kingsmere, PQ

"A NATION, LIKE AN INDIVIDUAL, TO FIND ITSELF MUST LOSE ITSELF IN THE SERVICE OF OTHERS."

King, 1927

As labour minister, King was concerned with working conditions in factories.

Marked for Success

King studied economics and law, and became an expert in industrial relations, the study of how employers and employees work together. In 1900 he was hired to run the government's new department of Labour. Because he did such good work, Sir Wilfrid Laurier asked him to run as an MP in the 1908 election. When King won, Laurier made him Labour minister.

Elected Leader

In 1919 the Liberals became the first political party to hold a leadership convention. King won the leadership race. In the 1921 election, he faced Arthur Meighen, an old opponent from his debating club days at university. King promised to lower the protective tariffs, or taxes, on U.S. goods, and said he'd bring in an old-age pension to help needy

senior citizens. Meighen was a better speaker than King, but voters preferred what King said and elected him PM.

A Small Majority, 1921–26

King didn't make many big changes at first. The Liberals held just one more seat than the Conservatives and the new Progressive Party combined. So King had to try to keep everybody happy. He cut the cost of shipping by freight train and lowered Canadian tariffs against American goods so the U.S. wouldn't object to buying Canadian wheat. As well, King paid back some of Canada's big loans from World War I. In 1925 he got the House of Commons to pass a bill giving needy Canadians over age 70 a pension of $20 per month, with the costs being shared by Ottawa and the provinces. But the bill was voted down in the Senate.

A Quebec "Lieutenant"

In 1921 King made a very wise decision: he brought MP Ernest Lapointe from Quebec into his Cabinet. King couldn't speak French, but he knew how important

it was to both the country and his party to understand the needs and wishes of French Canadians. For the next 20 years, Lapointe gave King excellent advice on what Quebec expected from the government.

In the Minority

After four years in office, King called an election. In October 1925, the Conservatives won 116 seats while King's Liberals held on to only 99. But King was able to stay on as PM with the support of the Progressives, who held 24 seats. However, if some Progressives turned against him, the other parties in the House could outvote him at any time. That nearly happened in June 1926.

World War II

Britain and France declared war on Germany on September 3, 1939, and with Parliament's approval, Canada joined the war on September 10. At the time, King promised there would be no conscription to force Canadians to fight in the war, though many chose to do so.

The war years, from 1939 to 1945, brought full employment and a huge business boom to Canada, but they also saw 1 000 000 brave Canadians sent overseas to fight. More than 42 000 lost their lives. The government raised taxes and borrowed money to fund the military. Food and gas rationing was introduced to ensure the troops were fed and their vehicles fuelled.

In 1942, afraid that some Japanese Canadians might not stay loyal to Canada, the government ordered them to leave their homes and live in special camps until the war was over. That same year, King held a special vote, or plebiscite, asking Canadians to release him from his promise not to force Canadians into military service overseas. Most Quebeckers voted against conscription, but an overall majority of Canadians said yes. King tried to make do with volunteers, but in late 1944 he agreed with military advisers that conscription was necessary.

Near war's end, Canada was among the countries working hard to set up the United Nations, an organization formed to encourage peace, security and cooperation among its members. When the war finally ended on August 14, 1945, Canadians were ready to begin the task of making peace, with King as their leader.

Smugglers found many clever ways to illegally carry liquor into the U.S.

The King-Byng Affair

In 1926 there was a law banning alcohol in the United States. At the time, dishonest Canadian customs officials were taking money from smugglers sneaking illegal liquor into the U.S. When the bribery became public, a majority of MPs, led by Opposition leader Meighen, called for a vote to show that the government couldn't be trusted any more. Knowing that a final vote would bring down his government, King asked Governor General Byng to dissolve Parliament instead and call a new election. Byng refused, King resigned, and Meighen was asked to form a new government. But Meighen's minority government was defeated by the Liberals and Progressives just three days later, and a new election had to be called after all.

DID YOU KNOW...

... King was Canada's longest-serving PM and the only one with a PhD?

OTHER MILESTONES

- *appointed the first woman, Cairine Wilson, to the Senate, 1930*
- brought in unemployment insurance, 1940
- brought in family allowances, 1944

In the Majority

After winning his third election in 1926, King brought back his old-age pension plan. This time the Senate passed the bill. That same year, he went to the Imperial Conference in England where he insisted that Canada was an independent country and that its parliament was the place where Canada's decisions about world affairs would be made.

But when some provincial premiers said Ottawa should give them money to help people who were out of work, King said he wouldn't help provinces run by Conservatives. Angry voters in those provinces turned to the Conservatives led by R.B. Bennett, and the Liberals were defeated in the 1930 election.

In Opposition

It was much easier being Opposition leader than PM during the Dirty Thirties when so many people were out of work (page 32). But King ran into trouble when an investigation showed that a company building a power project on the St. Lawrence River had contributed nearly $700 000 to the Liberal Party. King himself was accused of accepting a few hundred dollars, but his name was cleared. Humiliated, King promised the House he would clean up the Liberal Party, and went back to opposing Bennett's Conservatives.

Back as PM

When King returned to power in 1935 Canada badly needed a PM who could unite the country. The problems of the Great Depression still needed to be solved, and looming ahead was World War II. King was up to the challenge.

A Final Majority

In June 1945, King won a sixth election victory over the Conservatives (now the Progressive Conservatives). He stayed in office for another three years before retiring to his beloved home, Kingsmere, near Hull, PQ. King died in 1950. In his will, he left the 240-hectare (595-acre) Kingsmere estate as a gift to Canada.

King and his dog, Pat

Richard Bedford Bennett

> "CANADIANS HAVE A RIGHT TO A SYSTEM OF BROADCASTING FROM CANADIAN SOURCES EQUAL IN ALL RESPECTS TO THAT OF ANY OTHER COUNTRY."
>
> *Bennett, 1932*

Richard Bedford Bennett was born in New Brunswick and studied law in Nova Scotia. As a young lawyer, he moved to Calgary where he became a businessman and a millionaire. Bennett was a bit snobbish about his success. Because he had worked hard and done well, he thought everybody could. Still, he believed that rich people should give something back to their country. That's why he ran for Parliament and spent a lot of his money helping the Conservatives. In 1927 he became the first leader elected by Conservatives at the party's first leadership convention.

Hard Times

Bennett was ready and willing to form the government when King's Liberals lost in 1930. Unfortunately, he became prime minister during difficult times. During what was known as the Great Depression, thousands of Canadians were out of work, farmers were going broke, and businesses were closing because people had so little money to spend. Because Canada's trading partners, including the United States, had similar problems, they bought a lot less Canadian wheat, lumber, fish, and pulp and paper.

Quick Facts

Born: July 3, 1870, at Hopewell Hill, NB

Politics: Conservative

Occupation: teacher, lawyer

Political Positions: elected to North-West Territories Legislative Assembly, 1898; MP for Calgary East, AB, 1911–17; MP for Calgary West, 1925–39; leader of Conservatives, 1927–38

Prime Minister: Aug. 7, 1930–Oct. 23, 1935

Died: June 26, 1947, at Mickleham, Surrey, England

The Great Depression

By 1932, over 600 000 Canadians were out of work. Bad weather, a wheat fungus and grasshoppers plagued prairie farmers. Hungry people stood in soup lines to get free food. Thousands of men hopped on freight trains, "riding the rails" in search of jobs. Families were thrown out of their homes because they couldn't pay their bills. Anger and despair swept the country.

Looking for Answers

Bennett gave the provinces extra money to help the needy. The money was handed, or doled, out bit by bit, and people who needed it to get by were said to be "on the dole." Bennett also started a few government building projects to create more jobs, and set up some camps where unmarried men worked for 20¢ a day in exchange for food and a place to sleep.

Changing Course

But the Dirty Thirties just got dirtier. In 1935, an election year, Bennett created the Canadian Wheat Board to help farmers sell their wheat at decent prices. As well, Bennett did something else no other PM had done. He talked directly to Canadians through live radio broadcasts, telling them about his plans for Canada. Those broadcasts surprised even Conservatives. Bennett promised Canadians that he would introduce things he used to call bad ideas, such as a minimum wage and unemployment insurance.

Out and Away

But people remembered Bennett telling them that if they just worked harder, they wouldn't need so much help. And Conservatives thought he was trying to run the country all by himself. The fall election was a disaster. The Liberals won 171 of 245 seats, the Conservatives only 39. In 1938 an angry Bennett left politics. In 1939 he retired to England where some powerful friends arranged for him to sit in the British House of Lords. Bennett died in England in 1947.

DID YOU KNOW…

… Richard Bedford Bennett is the only PM not buried in Canada?

OTHER MILESTONES

- *set up the Canadian Radio Broadcasting Commission (later the CBC) to give Canadians their own radio stations and programs, 1932*
- *established the Bank of Canada to act as the federal government's banker, 1935*

Louis Stephen St. Laurent

In 1941 Louis St. Laurent was 59 years old and a successful business lawyer. He and his wife were enjoying their grandchildren and life was calm and comfortable. Suddenly, PM Mackenzie King was on the phone, asking St. Laurent to give all that up, and become his minister of Justice. Being a federal politician wasn't the most popular job for a Quebecker at the time. But when duty called, St. Laurent answered. "Uncle Louis" was on the way to becoming Canada's second French-Canadian prime minister.

> "I KNOW NOTHING OF POLITICS AND NEVER HAD ANYTHING TO DO WITH POLITICIANS."
>
> *St. Laurent, 1941*

Next in Line

King respected his clever Justice minister. In 1946, when countries were still sorting out the mess left by World War II, he put St. Laurent in charge of Canada's international relations. This was a first in Canada. Until then prime ministers had acted as their own ministers of External Affairs. Before retiring in 1948, King let Liberals know that St. Laurent was the man to replace him. They followed his advice, and in the 1949 election St. Laurent won a huge majority.

Getting Down to Business

In 1949, St. Laurent's government passed the Trans-Canada Highway Act, which offered the provinces a 50-50 split on the cost of building a highway from coast to coast. That same year, St. Laurent and Newfoundland government leader Joey Smallwood completed arrangements for Newfoundland to join Confederation on March 31. St. Laurent also oversaw Canada's joining the newly formed NATO (North Atlantic Treaty Organization) in April 1949.

Quick Facts

Born: Feb. 1, 1882, at Compton, PQ

Politics: Liberal

Married: Jeanne Renault, 1908 (five children)

Occupation: lawyer

Political Positions: MP for Quebec East, PQ, 1942–58; leader of Liberals, 1948–58

Prime Minister: Nov. 15, 1948–June 21, 1957

Died: July 25, 1973, at Quebec City, PQ

The Korean War

In 1950 Canada agreed to join an American-led United Nations force to keep North Korean communists from taking over South Korea. Over 300 Canadians died and 1200 were wounded by the end of the war in 1953. St. Laurent also agreed to send Canadians to Egypt as part of the UN's first peacekeeping force in 1956 (page 37).

The St. Lawrence Seaway

For some time, the U.S. and Canada had been talking about building the St. Lawrence Seaway to improve Great Lakes shipping, and St. Laurent wanted to get on with it. In 1951 he threatened to build all the new canals, locks and dams on the Canadian side of the river. That sped up the talks, and in 1954 the U.S. finally agreed to share costs and services. The seaway opened in April 1959.

Down the Pipe

In 1956 the Liberals proposed building a pipeline that would bring natural gas from Alberta to customers in the east. To speed their proposal through Parliament, the government set a time-limit on the debate in the House. The Conservatives said the Liberals had been in power so long that they didn't respect Parliament and the will of the people any more. St. Laurent's Liberals lost the next election. St. Laurent was 75 when he retired in January 1958. A few years later, he was asked his secret for staying so healthy. His answer: "Get defeated in an election."

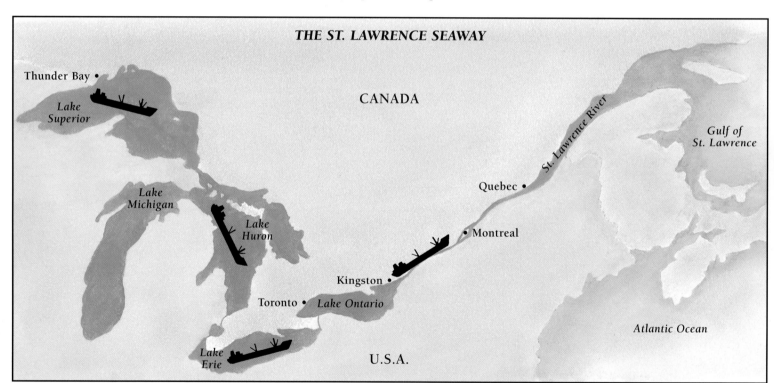

THE ST. LAWRENCE SEAWAY

Thunder Bay •

Lake Superior

CANADA

St. Lawrence River

Gulf of St. Lawrence

Lake Michigan

Lake Huron

Quebec •

Kingston •

Montreal •

Toronto • Lake Ontario

Atlantic Ocean

Lake Erie

U.S.A.

OTHER MILESTONES

- brought in the old-age pension to all people age 70 and over, and to those 65 to 69 who needed it, 1951
- *appointed the first Canadian-born governor general, Vincent Massey, 1952*
- established the National Library in Ottawa to preserve copies of materials published in Canada, 1953
- set up Canada's department of Northern Affairs, 1953

John George Diefenbaker

In July 1910, 14-year-old John Diefenbaker was selling newspapers at the Saskatoon railway station when Sir Wilfrid Laurier stepped down from a train. John sold him a paper, and the PM stopped to chat. After nearly half an hour, John said, "Well, Mr. Prime Minister, I can't waste any more time. I have to deliver my papers." Later, Laurier told an audience, "You have some remarkable news boys here." Nearly 50 years later, that "remarkable newsboy" would be prime minister.

Long Road to Power

Diefenbaker was known as an excellent lawyer when he first ran for Parliament in 1925. He lost that election and lost again in 1926, and in the provincial elections of 1929 and 1938. He finally took a seat in Parliament in 1940. Diefenbaker also ran twice for his party's leadership — in 1942 and 1948 — before winning in 1956. In June 1957, Diefenbaker led the Conservatives to their first victory in 27 years. But he didn't have a clear majority of seats in the House, so he called another election in 1958, and won the biggest majority ever — 208 of 265 seats.

Quick Facts

Born: Sept. 18, 1895, at Neustadt, ON

Politics: Conservative

Married: Edna Brower, 1929; widowed, 1951; married Olive Palmer, 1953 (one stepdaughter)

Occupation: lawyer

Political Positions: MP for Lake Centre, SK, 1940–53; MP for Prince Albert, SK, 1953–79; leader of Conservatives, 1956–67

Prime Minister: June 21, 1957–Apr. 22, 1963

Died: Aug. 16, 1979, at Ottawa, ON

"PARLIAMENT IS THE PLACE WHERE YOUR FREEDOM AND MINE IS MAINTAINED AND PRESERVED."

Diefenbaker, 1972

"Dief the Chief"

In his first election campaign as Conservative leader, Diefenbaker promised Canadians new roads, towns and mining jobs in the north, more help for farmers, better programs for the needy, and a bill of rights. But once in office, he had trouble making decisions and trusting his Cabinet ministers.

Fighting for Rights

Diefenbaker's proudest accomplishment came in 1960 when Parliament passed the Canadian Bill of Rights, to protect such basic human rights as freedom of speech and religion. As well, he gave all Aboriginal Canadians the same right to vote and to own property as other Canadians. The next year, he led the move to stop trade with South Africa until it ended its racist policies.

Problems, Problems

In 1959 Diefenbaker cancelled the development of a new fighter plane called the Avro Arrow. That decision

> **OTHER MILESTONES**
> • appointed the first woman Cabinet minister, Ellen Fairclough, 1957;
> first Aboriginal Canadian senator, James Gladstone, 1958;
> first French-Canadian governor general, Georges Vanier, 1959
> • brought in crop insurance for farmers, 1959
> • passed the Fitness and Amateur Sport Act
> giving money to amateur sports, 1961

put 14 000 people out of work. He also agreed to an American plan to set up a Canadian defence system that included nuclear missiles. In the 1962 election, his huge majority of seats in the House was reduced to a slim minority. Later that year, some people thought Diefenbaker was slow to put the armed forces on alert when President Kennedy ordered a blockade of Cuba to prevent it from accepting more Russian nuclear missiles. Criticism of Diefenbaker and his government grew louder.

Lost Confidence

In February 1963, after a vote that showed a majority of MPs had lost confidence in his government,

Diefenbaker was forced to call an election. The Liberals, led by Lester Pearson, were elected with a minority government.

In Opposition

As Opposition leader, Diefenbaker raged against Pearson's proposal for a new Canadian flag. He considered

it a rejection of the country's British roots. In the 1965 election, he held Pearson to another minority win. Many Conservatives began hinting that Diefenbaker should resign as party leader, but he refused. When they replaced him at the 1967 leadership convention, Diefenbaker felt as if he had been stabbed in the back. He stayed on as an MP until his death in 1979.

Avro Arrow

Lester Bowles Pearson

Lester Pearson loved wearing polka-dot bow ties. He also loved sports — he had played semi-pro baseball, coached university hockey and football, and was a lacrosse player and coach. Even when government business kept him busy, Pearson snatched every chance he could to take in a baseball game. And he always kept track of his favourite hockey team, the Toronto Maple Leafs.

> "ONLY MR. PEARSON COULD HAVE SAVED THE WORLD."
>
> *Nobel Prize Committee, 1957*

Public Service

For 20 years, Lester Pearson, better known as "Mike" — an air force nickname — worked as a diplomat, managing Canada's relationships with other nations. He was very involved in founding the North Atlantic Treaty Organization (page 33) and the United Nations (page 28), and he advised PM St. Laurent that Canada should support the UN and enter the Korean War (page 34).

Nobel Peace Prize

In 1956 Pearson proposed a way to end the fighting in Egypt over control of the Suez Canal. He convinced the UN to form an Emergency Force, which could be sent to trouble spots anywhere in the world, starting with Egypt. The next year he was awarded the Nobel Peace Prize for his efforts.

Slim Victories

Pearson replaced St. Laurent as Liberal leader in 1958 and led a minority government after both the 1963 and 1965 elections. He was able to push many major bills through Parliament with the support of New Democratic and Social Credit MPs.

Quick Facts

Born: Apr. 23, 1897, at Newtonbrook (now part of North York), ON

Politics: Liberal

Married: Maryon Moody, 1925 (two children)

Occupation: university history teacher, diplomat

Political Positions: MP for Algoma East, ON, 1948–68; leader of Liberals, 1958–68

Prime Minister: Apr. 22, 1963–Apr. 20, 1968

Died: Dec. 27, 1972, at Ottawa, ON

The "Bi and Bi" Commission

Quebeckers were feeling left out of political decisions and were growing more concerned about the need to protect their French language and culture. As well, new Canadians were struggling to keep their cultures alive. In 1963 Pearson set up the Royal Commission on Bilingualism and Biculturalism to study these problems and recommend ways to solve them.

A New Flag

In 1963 Pearson promised voters a new, distinctively Canadian flag. He met furious opposition from Conservative leader John Diefenbaker, and from Canadians who saw a new flag as a rejection of the country's British roots. But after months of bitter debate, the flag bill was finally passed in December 1964. On February 15, 1965, the new maple leaf flag flew for the first time over Parliament Hill.

1967: Celebrating 100 Years

Pearson hoped that a great birthday party celebrating Canada's centennial would bring Canadians together.

The party lasted all year. The highlight was Expo 67, the world's fair held in Montreal. Pearson also created the Order of Canada in 1967, an honour awarded to outstanding Canadians.

A Man of Peace

"Mike" Pearson retired from politics in April 1968 and died in 1972. Since 1979, the United Nations Association in Canada has given the Pearson Peace Medal to Canadians who follow Pearson's goal of trying to make the world more peaceful.

Canada's Pavilion at Expo 67

Pierre Elliott Trudeau

Pierre Elliott Trudeau was born into a well-to-do family, the son of a French-speaking father and an English-speaking mother. He was an independent young man who wasn't afraid to say what he thought. He liked judo, sky diving, skin diving and motorcycle riding, and he spent months backpacking around Europe and the Far East. Intelligent, charming and somewhat mysterious, Trudeau was the Liberals' choice to replace Pearson when he resigned as PM in 1968. Canadians would also be impressed when they met their new prime minister.

Quick Facts

Born: Oct. 18, 1919, at Montreal, PQ

Politics: Liberal

Married: Margaret Sinclair, 1971 (three children); divorced

Occupation: lawyer, law professor

Political Positions: MP for Mount Royal, PQ, 1965–84; leader of Liberals, 1968–84

Prime Minister: Apr. 20, 1968–June 3, 1979; Mar. 3, 1980–June 30, 1984

> "A COUNTRY IS NOT SOMETHING THAT IS BUILT, LIKE THE PHARAOHS BUILT THE PYRAMIDS AND LEFT STANDING THERE TO DEFY ETERNITY. A COUNTRY IS SOMETHING THAT IS BUILT EVERY DAY OUT OF CERTAIN BASIC VALUES."
>
> *Trudeau, 1984*

"Trudeaumania"

In the spring of 1968, crowds as large as 16 000 people, many of them still too young to vote, packed election rallies to see Trudeau. But they wanted to do more than just see him. They wanted to touch him, get his autograph and take home poster-sized pictures of him to hang on their walls. Canadians had never seen anything like it. They had just finished celebrating Canada's first 100 years as a nation. Could Trudeau lead them into the future? In the election held in June 1968, they decided he could.

Official Bilingualism

As justice minister in Pearson's Cabinet, Trudeau had made it very clear that he was against any special status or treatment for the province of Quebec. But he did believe that the federal government could do more to help all French-speaking Canadians feel at home in Canada. In 1969 he followed the advice of the "Bi and Bi" Commission (page 38), and passed the Official Languages Act. This act guaranteed that all Canadians could receive service from their federal government in both official languages.

Foreign Affairs

Trudeau didn't want Canada to be as involved in the problems of other countries as Pearson had. He cut in half the number of Canadian troops in the North Atlantic Treaty Organization (NATO) defence plan. He refused to interfere in a civil war in Nigeria. He also began to look for closer ties with countries other than

OTHER MILESTONES

• abolished capital punishment, 1976
• made a number of appointments that were firsts for women:
Muriel Fergusson, Speaker of the Senate, 1972;
Jeanne Sauvé, Speaker of the House of Commons, 1980;
Mme. Sauvé, governor general, 1984;
Bertha Wilson to the Supreme Court of Canada, 1982

the United States. These decisions pleased some people and upset others.

Election, Election

Trudeau called an election in the fall of 1972. By then Canadians knew their PM better, and they either loved him or wanted him out of office. He won again, but with a minority government. In the next two years, prices kept rising, workers kept asking for raises, and many people couldn't find jobs. The Conservatives asked Trudeau to put limits on both prices and wages, but he refused. In May 1974, a majority of MPs voted against the government, and Trudeau was forced to call another election. This time the Liberals won a clear majority.

Challenging Times

In October 1975, Trudeau finally put limits on the raises of wage-earners and the profits of businesses. In 1976 the Parti Québécois, led by René Lévesque, promised to fight for Quebec's independence, and won a big majority in a Quebec election. That moved Trudeau to speak out more than ever against independence for Quebec. Trudeau also spoke out at the United Nations against countries looking to build or buy nuclear weapons.

The October Crisis

In the 1960s, members of a revolutionary group calling itself the FLQ (Front de Libération du Québec) turned to violence to show how much they wanted Quebec to be independent from Canada. They terrorized Montrealers with over 200 bombings, and in October 1970 they kidnapped two hostages: a British trade official, James Cross (left), and Quebec's Labour minister, Pierre Laporte (right). People in Quebec and the rest of Canada were frightened about what was happening.

When the Quebec government asked Ottawa to send soldiers to Montreal to protect people, Trudeau agreed. He also used a special law, the Emergency War Measures Act to allow police to jail suspects immediately, without following the usual rules for arresting people. The next day, the kidnappers murdered Pierre Laporte. The police captured Laporte's murderers, and the FLQ finally released James Cross on December 3, in exchange for a flight to Cuba.

Calm returned to Montreal, and most of the people jailed under the War Measures Act were released without being charged. Some people thought Trudeau had over-reacted, some were very angry because he had taken away Canadians' basic freedoms, and some thought it was good that he had acted so swiftly and firmly. The disagreement among Canadians about how Trudeau should have handled the October Crisis continues to this day.

Goodbye, Hello

Trudeau resigned as party leader in November 1979. But when Clark's minority government was defeated a month later (page 44), he agreed to return as leader to fight the election that was just two months away. The Liberals were happy he did, because they won again.

Battling for Canada

In the months following his re-election, Trudeau was often in his home province, urging Quebeckers to choose to remain part of Canada in a special vote, or referendum, to be held in Quebec on May 20, 1980. Trudeau's side won. After the referendum, he began to plan the one thing he wanted most — to give Canadians their own Constitution, one that could be changed in Canada instead of in Britain and that would include basic rights and freedoms guaranteed by law.

Liberal Loss

The Liberals ended the controls on prices and wages in 1978, but by 1979, many unemployed people and struggling farmers had given up on the Liberals. Financial experts complained that the government was still spending too much and increasing Canada's debts. When an election was called that year, the winners were the Conservatives, led by Joe Clark, who had promised jobs and lower taxes.

DID YOU KNOW...

... Trudeau won the Albert Einstein Peace Prize in 1984? He received it for his efforts to rid the world of nuclear weapons and make it a more peaceful place.

A New Constitution

In October 1980, Trudeau went on TV to announce his constitutional plans. After a year of hot debate, the premiers of nine provinces finally agreed to the constitutional changes. Quebec's premier didn't, and he refused to sign the agreement. Nevertheless, the new Constitution Act and the Charter of Rights and Freedoms became law on April 17, 1982.

> "LIVING NEXT TO YOU [THE U.S.] IS IN SOME WAYS LIKE SLEEPING WITH AN ELEPHANT. NO MATTER HOW FRIENDLY OR EVEN-TEMPERED IS THE BEAST … ONE IS AFFECTED BY EVERY TWITCH AND GRUNT."
>
> *Trudeau, 1969*

The End of an Era

In 1978 Trudeau had told the United Nations that countries should refuse to test missiles and planes designed to carry nuclear weapons. But in 1983 the Liberal government agreed to allow the United States to test some of these missiles in northern Canada. Later that year, and on into early 1984, Trudeau visited many world leaders in an effort to convince them to reduce the stock of nuclear weapons. Then, on February 29, 1984, he announced to Canadians that he was resigning again. Trudeau returned to private life and began writing books and practising law. But he remained a very powerful voice in Canada. He spoke out against the Meech Lake Accord and the Charlottetown Accord, two plans designed to give more power to the provinces and special treatment to Quebec (page 48).

Queen Elizabeth signing the Constitution Act

Charles Joseph Clark

When Joe Clark was 16, he won a local public-speaking contest. His prize? A trip to Canada's capital, including a visit to Parliament Hill. Clark enjoyed Ottawa, but he didn't like all the shouting and heckling in the House of Commons. But 17 years later, he proudly took his seat in that noisy House as MP for Rocky Mountain, AB. And less than four years later, he ran for the leadership of the Conservative Party.

"Joe Who?" Joe Clark!

When Clark won the Conservative leadership in 1976, most Canadians had never heard of him. When the gutsy newcomer ran against Pierre Trudeau in 1979, newspaper headlines asked, "Joe who?" While voters hardly knew Clark, they did know Trudeau, and many thought it was time for a change. After 16 years in Opposition, the Conservatives were back in power and Joe Clark was PM.

In the Minority

After choosing his Cabinet, which included Lincoln Alexander, Canada's first black Cabinet minister, Clark waited over four months to call Parliament back. He spent that time getting prepared. When Trudeau resigned as Liberal leader in November, Clark felt confident about leading his minority government.

Letting Power Slip Away

Clark's budget included taxes that would send oil and gas prices soaring. Opposition MPs prepared to vote against the government. Never dreaming he could lose, Clark didn't make sure that all his MPs were present in the House for the vote. He lost by three votes. Stunned, he called an election for February 1980, and lost to Trudeau. Clark spent three years as Opposition leader, then lost a leadership race to Brian Mulroney. He remained an MP until the 1993 election wiped out all but two Conservative MPs.

John Napier Turner

John Turner was just two when his father died. To support her family, his mother took a government job in Ottawa, where life for the Turners included having politicians as neighbours and friends. Young John would chat with Lester Pearson, and nod to PM King when they walked their dogs. In high school, Turner was a scholarship student and track athlete. He won Canadian junior and senior sprinting championships, and was preparing to try out for the 1948 Olympics when a car accident ended that dream. But his dream of serving as PM would come true, if only for a little while.

If Trudeau Hadn't ...

If Pierre Trudeau hadn't run for the Liberal leadership in 1968, Turner might have become PM then. He was popular and fluently bilingual. Instead, Turner became Trudeau's Justice minister and, later, Finance minister. After he argued with Trudeau over some finance issues in 1975, Turner resigned and returned to law.

If Turner Hadn't ...

Turner returned to politics when Trudeau resigned in 1984. He beat Jean Chrétien in the Liberal leadership race, and was sworn in as PM. Knowing he would have to fight

Quick Facts

Born: June 7, 1929, at Richmond, Surrey, England

Politics: Liberal

Married: Geills McCrae Kilgour, 1963 (four children)

Occupation: lawyer

Political Positions: MP for St. Laurent-St. Georges, PQ, 1962–68; MP for Ottawa-Carleton, ON, 1968–76; MP for Vancouver Quadra, BC, 1984–93; leader of Liberals, 1984–90

Prime Minister: June 30, 1984–Sept. 17, 1984

an election soon, he called one right away. In a TV debate, Opposition leader Brian Mulroney attacked Turner for going along with Trudeau's plan to give government jobs to so many retiring MPs. A majority of voters agreed with Mulroney, and the Conservatives won the election.

So Little Time

Turner lasted only 79 days, the second-shortest term for any prime minister. He stayed on as Opposition leader, fighting Mulroney's free-trade plans until he retired from politics in 1990.

Martin Brian Mulroney

When he was only 13, Brian Mulroney was already telling his friends in Baie-Comeau that he wanted to be prime minister one day. Although the Liberals were popular in his home province of Quebec, Mulroney became involved with the Conservatives as a high-school student in New Brunswick. He was popular with his classmates, and his circle of friends from Baie-Comeau and New Brunswick grew to include friends he met in Quebec City while studying law at Laval University. Many of them would help him when he decided to run for the leadership of the Conservative Party.

On the Move

Mulroney was 36 and a successful lawyer when he decided to enter politics. In 1976 he jumped right in and joined the Conservative leadership race. Joe Clark won, but many people now knew Mulroney's name. He became president of the Iron Ore Company of Canada, but in 1983 Mulroney left the company and returned to his law practice. Later that year, he ran for the leadership of the Conservative Party again, and this time he won. Mulroney finally gained a seat in Parliament after winning a by-election.

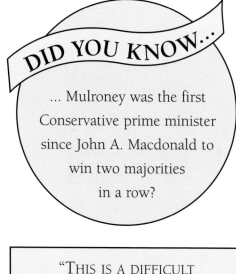

Quick Facts

Born: Mar. 20, 1939, at Baie-Comeau, PQ

Politics: Conservative

Married: Mila Pivnicki, 1973 (four children)

Occupation: lawyer, businessman

Political Positions: leader of Conservatives, 1983–93; MP for Central Nova, NS, 1983–84; MP for Manicouagan, PQ, 1984–88; MP for Charlevoix, PQ, 1988–93

Prime Minister: Sept. 17, 1984–June 25, 1993

DID YOU KNOW...

... Mulroney was the first Conservative prime minister since John A. Macdonald to win two majorities in a row?

"THIS IS A DIFFICULT COUNTRY TO GOVERN."
Mulroney, 1986

Landslide Victory

When the next federal election was called in 1984, many Canadians were out of work, the Liberal government was borrowing more money, and interest in independence was growing in Quebec. People wanted a change from the Liberals. In his campaign, Mulroney promised to cut spending without touching benefits, such as old-age pensions. He also promised jobs and a way to deal with Quebec's concerns. Mulroney was the clear winner against John Turner in a TV debate, and led the Conservatives to a huge victory on election day.

Grey Power

When the Conservatives brought in their first budget, Finance minister Michael Wilson said he could save $650 million. But it meant cutting back on old-age pension increases. Senior citizens were furious. They held protest meetings and marched on Parliament Hill in Ottawa. Mulroney forced Wilson to back down and decided the government should raise money by increasing taxes on businesses and gas, instead of cutting back on pensions.

Tuna Troubles

Some Cabinet ministers were forced to resign because of scandals during Mulroney's first years as PM. The scandal that upset most Canadians involved canned tuna that health inspectors said wasn't fit to be eaten. The Fisheries minister let the tuna be sold anyway so that fish plant workers wouldn't lose their jobs.

Agreements and Disagreements

In 1986 Mulroney decided it was time to change the Constitution in a way that would satisfy Quebec (page 43). He met with the provincial premiers in April 1987 at Meech Lake, near Ottawa. When the meeting ended, Mulroney proudly announced that an accord, or agreement, had been reached and that the premiers had three years to get the approval of their provincial legislatures.

Try as he might, Mulroney couldn't stop the accord from falling apart. Critics pointed out problems with the deal, and in May 1987, former PM Pierre Trudeau said it was a terrible plan that would weaken Canada by giving the provinces too much power. His words worried many English-speaking Canadians and angered many Quebeckers. Mulroney's plan to unite Canada was doing the opposite. In the end, two provinces didn't give their approval, and the Meech Lake Accord died.

In 1992 Mulroney again tried to find a deal that would make French-speaking Quebeckers feel more secure. He met with the provincial premiers in Charlottetown, PEI. With former prime minister Joe Clark's help, he worked out a new agreement known as the Charlottetown Accord. This time, Mulroney asked all Canadians to vote on it in a special referendum. Aboriginal people and voters in seven provinces, including Quebec, rejected the accord.

Capital Punishment

Several Conservatives and many Canadians wanted to bring back the death penalty for certain types of murders. Mulroney disagreed, but he allowed his MPs to vote according to their personal beliefs on the new capital punishment bill introduced in 1987. The other party leaders did the same, and the bill was defeated.

Free Trade

In 1983 Mulroney said he didn't support free trade between Canada and the U.S. But in 1984, he told American business leaders that Canada was "open for business again." He encouraged them to set up shop in Canada, hoping this would create jobs. In 1985 Mulroney announced that he wanted to work out a deal with the U.S. that would cut the special taxes that each country put on the other's products

Mulroney and U.S. President Ronald Reagan

when they crossed the border. Most Canadian business experts thought free trade was a good idea, but union leaders argued that many jobs would disappear.

Winning the Free-Trade Debate

Mulroney succeeded in working out the free-trade deal. But before it was finally signed, he called an election. Mulroney won another majority, and the trade agreement went into effect on January 1, 1989.

Popularity Plunges

In 1991 the Mulroney government brought in a new tax on most goods and services sold in Canada. Known as the Goods and Services Tax (GST), it was very unpopular. Many Canadians were also angry because the free-trade deal hadn't brought the new jobs Mulroney had promised. By early 1993, opinion polls showed that Mulroney was the most unpopular PM in Canadian history. He resigned that spring as Conservative leader, and in the next federal election his party won only two seats.

OTHER MILESTONES

- sent Canadian forces to join the American-led Gulf War against Iraq, 1991
- signed the North American Free Trade Agreement (NAFTA), 1992
- *reached a settlement with the Inuit in the Northwest Territories to form a new territory called Nunavut, 1993*

Avril Kim Campbell

As a teenager, Kim Campbell dared to think that one day she would become prime minister. She tested her political wings in high school. No girl at her school had ever been elected student council president, but Campbell ran and won. And at university, she became the first female president of her first-year class.

Rookie MP from B.C.

Campbell's election as a member of Parliament in 1988 was a close call. She won by less than 300 votes. Although most new MPs usually wait a few years before getting Cabinet posts, PM Mulroney made Campbell minister of Indian Affairs right away. The next year, he gave her the job of minister of Justice, and in 1993 she became minister of National Defence and Veterans Affairs.

Canada's First Female PM

Campbell did well, but by the early 1990s, Mulroney was very unpopular and so was his party. When he resigned as leader of the Conservative Party in 1993, Campbell quickly entered the race to replace him. She won, and took over as PM.

The Party's Over

Campbell's triumph was short-lived. It had been nearly five years since the last election, and it was time for another one. In her election campaign, Campbell promised a "new way of doing politics," but voters didn't care. They just wanted to get rid of the Conservatives. Only two Conservatives were elected in 1993, and Campbell wasn't one of them.

> ### Quick Facts
>
> Born: Mar. 10, 1947, at Port Alberni, BC
>
> Politics: Conservative
>
> Married: (later divorced from) Nathan Divinsky, 1972; married (later divorced from) Howard Eddy, 1986 (no children)
>
> Occupation: lawyer, university lecturer
>
> Political Positions: member of BC's Legislative Assembly, 1986; MP for Vancouver Centre, 1988–93; leader of Conservatives, June 13, 1993–Dec. 13, 1993
>
> Prime Minister: June 25, 1993–Nov. 4, 1993

DID YOU KNOW...

... Campbell was the first woman to serve as Canada's attorney general?

Joseph Jacques Jean Chrétien

Jean Chrétien, the "little guy from Shawinigan," grew up in a large, loving family. His parents saved every extra cent to make sure all their children got the best education they could afford. Chrétien was sent away to boarding school when he was five. Though he was a good student, he missed his parents and found the school's discipline too strict. He also had to cope with being teased about his deafness in one ear and the paralysis on the left side of his face, which had been caused by a childhood illness.

Political Ambitions

Chrétien studied law because he knew most winning politicians were lawyers. He was just 29 when he became an MP in 1963. Chrétien headed off to Ottawa, speaking hardly any English. After holding four other Cabinet posts, he realized his dream of becoming the first French-Canadian Finance minister in September 1977

> **Quick Facts**
>
> *Born: Jan. 11, 1934, at Shawinigan, PQ*
>
> *Politics: Liberal*
>
> *Married: Aline Chaîné, 1957 (three children)*
>
> *Occupation: lawyer*
>
> *Political Positions: MP for Saint-Maurice–Laflèche, PQ, 1963–68; MP for Saint-Maurice, PQ, 1968–86; MP for Beauséjour, NB, 1990–93; leader of Liberals, 1990– ; MP for Saint-Maurice, PQ, 1993–*
>
> *Prime Minister: Nov. 4, 1993–*

Gone and Back Again

In 1986, two years after losing the race to become leader of the Liberal Party, Chrétien took a break from politics. He returned in 1990 and won his party's leadership. After winning a by-election a few months later, Chrétien was back in the House of Commons as leader of the Opposition.

> "I ALWAYS CONCLUDE MY SPEECHES WITH ONE PLAIN TRUTH: CANADA IS THE BEST!"
>
> *Chrétien, 1990*

... Jean Chrétien's most trusted adviser is his wife, Aline?

Swept into Office

Chrétien had always been a very popular politician. People saw him as honest, friendly and down-to-earth. He was very proud to be a French Canadian, and he loved his country deeply. When he went up against the Conservatives in the 1993 election, memories of Brian Mulroney were still very fresh in voters' minds. Canadians wanted a break from trying to fix the Constitution. They also thought Chrétien was going to get rid of the hated GST (page 49).

New Players in Parliament

Chrétien won a large majority, and the Conservatives won only two seats. Two new parties, the Reform Party and the Bloc Québécois, arrived in Ottawa with over 100 seats between them, and the Bloc became the official Opposition.

Smooth Sailing on Rough Waters

With Chrétien as PM, Canadians seemed to be more willing to put up with the spending cuts the government made to try to balance its budget. Many weren't happy that

unemployment stayed high and that Chrétien didn't get rid of the GST. But his popularity remained high.

Fears for the Country

The most difficult time for Chrétien and all Canadians came in October 1995, when Quebeckers voted on whether or not to separate from Canada. Chrétien was convinced that a majority of Quebeckers would choose Canada over independence, and advised people outside Quebec to remain calm. Even when opinion polls showed the vote might be close, Chrétien felt he shouldn't interfere. On October 30, a very slim majority voted against separation.

A Second Term

In the spring of 1997, after three-and-a-half years in office, Chrétien called an election. Some voters were angry that he had kept the GST, and many were worried that he didn't have a plan ready if Quebeckers voted again on the issue of separation. But a slim majority gave Chrétien's Liberals another chance.

OTHER MILESTONES
• led Team Canada, made up of provincial premiers and business leaders, on three trips to other countries to create new trade deals for Canada, 1994–97
• passed new gun control laws, 1996

Time Line

Prime Ministers		Events
Sir John A. Macdonald		
1867–1873	1867	• Dominion of Canada formed
	1869	• The Red River Rebellion
Alexander Mackenzie		
1873–1878	1873	• The North-West Mounted Police formed
	1874	• The secret ballot method of voting brought in
	1875	• The Supreme Court set up
Sir John A. Macdonald		
1878–1891	1878	
	1885	• The last spike driven in the cross-Canada railway
Sir John Abbott		
1891–1892	1891	
Sir John Thompson		
1892–1894	1892	• Criminal Code bill passed
Sir Mackenzie Bowell		
1894–1896	1894	
Sir Charles Tupper		
1896	1896	• Gold discovered in the Klondike
Sir Wilfrid Laurier		
1896–1911	1896	
	1899	• The South African (Boer) War begins
	1902	• The South African (Boer) War ends
Sir Robert Borden		
1911–1920	1911	
	1914	• World War I begins
	1917	• Income tax brought in
	1918	• Women receive the right to vote in federal elections
		• World War I ends
	1919	• The Winnipeg General Strike
Arthur Meighen		
1920–1921	1920	
Mackenzie King		
1921–1926	1921	
Arthur Meighen		
1926	1926	
Mackenzie King		
1926–1930	1926	
	1929	• The Great Depression begins
Richard Bennett		
1930–1935	1930	
Mackenzie King		
1935–1948	1935	

Prime Ministers		Events
	1939	• World War II begins
		• The Great Depression ends
	1940	• Unemployment insurance brought in
	1944	• Family allowance brought in
	1945	• World War II ends
Louis St. Laurent		
1948–1957	1948	
	1950	• The Korean War begins
	1953	• The Korean War ends
		• Department of Northern Affairs set up
John Diefenbaker		
1957–1963	1957	
	1959	• The St. Lawrence Seaway opens
	1960	• Canadian Bill of Rights passed
Lester Pearson		
1963–1968	1963	• The Royal Commission on Bilingualism and Biculturalism set up
	1965	• Canada gets its Maple Leaf flag
		• Canada Pension Plan set up
	1966	• Medical Care Act (Medicare) passed
	1967	• Canada's centennial year
Pierre Trudeau		
1968–1979	1968	
	1969	• The Official Languages Act passed
	1970	• The October Crisis
	1976	• Capital punishment abolished
Joe Clark		
1979–1980	1979	
Pierre Trudeau		
1980–1984	1980	• The first referendum about Quebec separation held
	1982	• The new Constitution Act and the Charter of Rights and Freedoms become law
John Turner		
1984	1984	
Brian Mulroney		
1984–1993	1984	
	1989	• The Free-Trade Agreement goes into effect
	1991	• The Goods and Services Tax (GST) brought in
Kim Campbell		
1993	1993	
Jean Chrétien		
1993–	1993	
	1999	• Nunavut is formed

53

Index

A

Abbott, John, 15, 16, 18
Aboriginal peoples, 10, 36, 48
Albert Einstein Peace Prize, 42
Alberta, 22
Alexander, Lincoln, 44
auditor generals, 14
Auto Pact, 38
Avro Arrow, 36

B

Bank of Canada, 32
Bennett, Richard, 30, 31-32
Bilingualism and Biculturalism, 38, 40
Bill of Rights, 36
bills, 6
Bloc Québécois, 52
Boer War, 21
Borden, Robert, 22, 23-24, 25
Bowell, Mackenzie, 17, 18
British Columbia, 11, 14
British Commonwealth, 24

C

Cabinet, 5, 6, 7
Campbell, Kim, 50
Canada East, 9
Canada Pension Plan, 38
Canada West, 9
Canadian Bill of Rights, 36
Canadian National Railway, 25
Canadian Pacific Railway, 11, 12, 14, 18
Canadian Radio Broadcasting Commission, 32
Canadian Wheat Board, 32
capital punishment, 40, 49
Centennial, 38
Charlottetown Conference, 9
Charlottetown Accord, 43, 48
Charter of Rights and Freedoms, 43
Chrétien, Jean, 45, 51-52
Clark, Joseph, 42, 44, 46, 48
Confederation, 9, 18. *See also* 9 (New Brunswick, Nova Scotia, Ontario, Quebec), 10 (Manitoba, Northwest Territories), 11 (British Columbia, Prince Edward Island), 22 (Alberta, Saskatchewan, Yukon Territory), 33 (Newfoundland)

conscription, 22, 24, 25, 28
Conservative Party, 4, 31
Constitution, 6, 42, 43, 48
criminal code, 16
crop insurance, 36
Cross, James, 41
Cuban missile crisis, 36

D

democracy, 4
departments, government, 5
    of External Affairs, 20, 33
    of Labour, 20, 27
    of Northern Affairs, 34
Diefenbaker, John, 35-36, 38
Dirty Thirties, 30, 32

E

elections, 4, 6, 24
Emergency War Measures Act, 24, 41
Employment Service of Canada, 24
Expo 67, 38

F

Fairclough, Ellen, 36
family allowances, 29
Fathers of Confederation, 9, 18
federal elections, 4, 6, 24
Fergusson, Muriel, 40
Fitness and Amateur Sport Act, 36
flag debate, 36, 38
free trade, 14, 22, 23, 45, 49
Front de Libération du Québec (FLQ), 41

G

Gladstone, James, 36
Goods and Service Tax (GST), 49, 52
government, Canadian, 4-7
governor general, 4, 34, 36, 40
Great Depression, 30, 31, 32
Gulf War, 49
gun control, 52

H

head of state, 4
House of Commons, 5, 7
Houses of Parliament, 5
Hudson's Bay Company, 11

I

Imperial Conference, 30
income tax, 24
Inuit, 49

J

Japanese Canadians, 28

K

King-Byng Affair, 29
King, Mackenzie, 25, 26-30, 31, 33, 45
Kingsmere, 30
Klondike gold rush, 22
Korean War, 34, 37

L

Lapointe, Ernest, 27
Laporte, Pierre, 41
Last Spike, 12
Laurier, Wilfrid, 18, 19-22, 23, 27, 35
leadership conventions,
    first Liberal, 27
    first Conservative, 31
League of Nations, 24
legislation, 5
Lévesque, René, 40
Liberal Party, 4, 27
liquor smuggling, 25, 29

M

Macdonald, John A., 8-12, 14, 15, 16, 17, 18, 46
Mackenzie, Alexander, 13-14
Mackenzie, William Lyon, 26
Manitoba, 10, 17, 18, 21
Maple Leaf flag, 38
Massey, Vincent, 34
Medicare (Medical Care Act), 38
Meech Lake Accord, 43, 48
Meighen, Arthur, 25, 27, 29
members of Parliament, 4, 7
Métis, 10
minimum wage, 32
ministers, Cabinet, 5
Mulroney, Brian, 44, 45, 46-49, 50, 52

N

National Library, 34
national park, first, 12
New Brunswick, 9
Newfoundland, 9, 33
Nobel Peace Prize, 37
North American Free Trade
    Agreement (NAFTA), 49
North Atlantic Treaty Organization
    (NATO), 33, 37, 40
North-West Mounted Police, 12,
    14, 20
Northwest Territories, 10, 11, 49
Nova Scotia, 9, 18
Nunavut, 49

O

October Crisis, 41
Official Languages Act, 40
old-age pensions, 27, 30, 34, 47
Ontario, 9
Opposition, 5
Order of Canada, 38

P

Pacific Railway Scandal, 11, 14
park, first national, 12
parliament, 5, 6
Parti Québécois, 40
Pearson, Lester, 36, 37-38, 39,
    40, 45
Pearson Peace Medal, 38
pipeline debate, 34
plebiscite, 28

political parties, 4, 7. *See also* Bloc
    Québécois, Conservative Party,
    Liberal Party, Parti Québécois,
    Progressive Party, Reform Party
price and wage controls, 40
prime minister, 4-5, 6-7
Prince Edward Island, 9, 11
Progressive Party, 25, 27

Q

Quebec, 9, 10, 38, 40, 41, 42, 43,
    47, 48, 52
Quebec referendum
    of 1980, 42
    of 1995, 52

R

radio broadcasts, 32
reciprocity, 23
Red River Rebellion, 10
Reform Party, 52
Riel, Louis, 10, 18
royal assent, 6
Royal Canadian Mounted Police
    (RCMP), 12, 24
Royal Canadian Navy, 20, 22, 23
Rupert's Land, 11

S

Saskatchewan, 10, 22
Sauvé, Jeanne, 40
secret ballot, 14
Senate, 5, 6
Smallwood, Joey, 33
St. Laurent, Louis, 33-34, 37

St. Lawrence Seaway, 34
Supreme Court, 6, 14

T

Taché, Etienne-Paschal, 9
tariffs, 14, 27
Thompson, John, 15, 16, 18
trade unions, 12
Trans-Canada Highway Act, 33
Trudeau, Pierre, 39-43, 44, 45, 48
tuna, tinned, 47
Tupper, Charles, 18, 23
Turner, John, 45, 47

U

unemployment insurance, 29, 32
Union Government, 24
United Nations, 28, 34, 37, 40, 43
United Nations Association in
    Canada, 38

V

Vanier, Georges, 36
voting rights, women's, 24

W

Wilson, Bertha, 40
Wilson, Cairine, 29
Wilson, Michael, 47
Winnipeg General Strike, 24, 25
World War I, 22, 24, 27
World War II, 28, 33

Y

Yukon Territory, 22

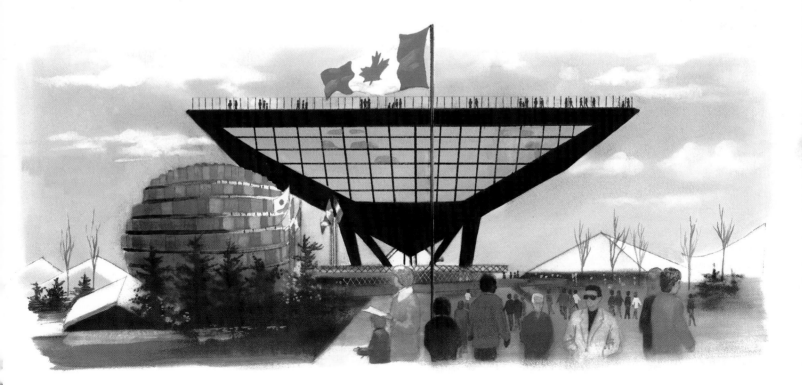

Artwork rendered in oil wash and pencil

Text set in Berkeley

Printed in Hong Kong by Wing King Tong Company Limited

Primary sources for information in this book included
The Canadian Encyclopedia (second edition), *Dictionary of Canadian Biography*
and *The Junior Encyclopedia of Canada*